Playing in a Band

By Diane Church

Photographs by Chris Fairclough

W
FRANKLIN WATTS
NEW YORK • LONDON • SYDNEY

Matt and Dom are best friends. They play in the local band together. Dom has asthma, which means he sometimes finds it hard to breathe. In the picture, Dom is on the right.

Tonight the boys have a band practice and Matt is staying at Dom's house for the night.

Asthma is very common. Every year the number of people with asthma goes up.

It's the end of the school day. Dom's mum collects him from the gate. "It's going to be brilliant having Matt to stay tonight!" Dom tells her.

Having asthma doesn't stop Dom doing things he enjoys such as playing the cornet in the band and spending time with his friends.

At home, Dom plays football in the garden with his brothers.
They often play football after school.
"Pass the ball to me!" shouts Dom.

Sport is good for people who have asthma as it helps to make their lungs strong.

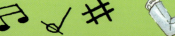

At 6 o'clock,
Dom's mum
drives him
to the band hall.
"Have you
done your
practice?"
she asks.
"Yes, it's a
really difficult
piece," Dom
replies.

Playing the cornet
in the band helps
Dom to control his
breathing during
an asthma attack.
If he has an attack,
he knows how to
keep his breathing
even and calm.

Dom carries his cornet in a case.
"Can you manage?" asks his mum.
"Of course!" Dom tells her.

Inside the hall Matt is waiting for his friend. The boys polish their cornets before the rehearsal.

"Hello, everyone!" says Maureen, the band leader. "We'll start in two minutes."
"I've played a lot this week!" Matt tells Maureen. Sometimes the boys have difficulty finding enough time to practise.

The band plays the piece the boys have been practising. But Dom has trouble playing as well as he wants to.
"My asthma is making me cough," he thinks.
"I can't take a deep enough breath."

An asthma attack can be triggered by different things such as having a cold, traffic fumes, pollen and cigarette smoke.

"Are you O.K?" Maureen asks Dom.
"I think it's the weather," he tells her.
"It's so damp outside it's making it hard
for me to breathe deeply."
"Just take it gently then, Dom," says Maureen.

> Dom finds it hard to breathe if
> the weather is too hot or too cold,
> or if it is very damp.

Dom does his best to breathe deeply
and plays his cornet well.
"That was wonderful!" Maureen
congratulates them all. "See you next week!"

"That was really good!" Matt tells Dom.
"Thanks!" says Dom.
The boys are hungry after their practice.
"I'm starving! Shall we get something
to eat?" Dom asks.

Dom's mum suggests they have fish and chips. "Yummy!" laughs Matt. "We hardly ever have take-aways!" "This is a special treat for us too!" Dom's mum tells the boys.

After they have eaten they all go home. Dom takes Matt to his room. "What are these?" asks Matt. Dom explains that they are puffers, or inhalers, for his asthma.

Dom has two puffers. He uses them every morning and evening. The brown one is called a preventer. The blue one is a reliever. Dom uses the reliever when he feels he is about to have an asthma attack

There is just time for a game of snooker
before the boys go to bed. "I'll beat you
any day!" Matt warns Dom. Matt is good at
snooker and he wins.

In bed Dom's chest feels tight. "It's so hot tonight," he complains to Matt. "I'd better use my reliever." But, later in the night, Dom starts wheezing badly.

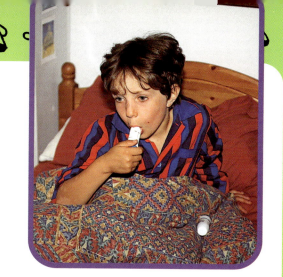

When Dom is asleep he doesn't control his breathing as well as when he is awake so he may be more likely to have an asthma attack.

Dom wakes up. He is having an asthma attack. "Stay calm, Dom," Matt tells him. "I'll get your mum."

If you are with someone when they have an asthma attack, keep calm and help them to breathe slowly. They need their reliever. Tell an adult.

Dom's mum helps Dom to find his reliever and control his breathing.
"I can't believe I had an attack," Dom reassures Matt.
"I hardly ever have one!"
The boys soon go back to sleep.

Dom feels better after using his reliever. If his breathing doesn't get better after ten minutes he has to go to hospital. A bad attack can be dangerous.

At breakfast, the boys talk about the day ahead. "Thanks for having me to stay," Matt says. "No problem, next time I'll beat you at snooker though!" Dom tells his friend.

Then Dom gets his bag
ready for school.
"I won't forget my
puffer, Mum!" he promises.

Dom takes his puffers with him everywhere he goes. The teachers at school know Dom has asthma and how to help if he has an attack.

Facts about people with asthma

★ People with asthma can do many of the same things as other people — they just have to think about their breathing more than others.

★ Asthma is very common — the number of people with asthma is increasing every year.

★ Asthma can be controlled with special medicines.

★ When someone has an asthma attack, the airways that carry the air in and out of their body become swollen, making it difficult for them to breathe.

★ An asthma attack is usually set off, or triggered, by something such as having a cold or infection, traffic fumes, pollen, fur or the weather. Very hot or very cold weather can affect people with asthma.

★ Exercise is good for people with asthma as it makes their lungs healthier and stronger.

Glossary

airways   the tubes that take air in and out of your body.

asthma   a condition which means that sometimes you find it hard to breathe.

pollen   tiny particles that are given off by plants and flowers.

puffer or inhaler   there are two types of inhaler, a preventer which is usually brown, and a reliever which is usually blue. The person takes a deep breath using their inhaler and lets it out slowly. The medicine goes into their lungs and helps them breathe easier.

Try to be helpful

★ **1.** If you are with someone when they have an asthma attack, do not panic. Keep calm and get them to sit up straight and take their reliever.

★ **2.** Talk to the person and try to calm them down.

★ **3.** Tell an adult. If their inhaler is not helping them after 5-10 minutes and it is a serious attack you may have to call 999 for an ambulance.

★ **4.** If you have a friend with asthma, make sure you know where they keep their puffers. They will need to use the blue one if they have an attack.

★ **5.** Be considerate. Someone with asthma can do most of the things you do, but sometimes they need extra time to take their puffers.

Further information and addresses

National Asthma Campaign
and Junior Asthma Club (for children
aged 4-13 years with asthma and their friends)
Providence House
Providence Place
London
N1 0NT
Asthma Helpline 0845 7 01 02 03 (Mon-Fri 9 a.m.— 7 p.m.)
Website: http/www.asthma.org.uk

REACH National Advice Centre for
Children with Reading Difficulties
Nine Mile Ride
California Country Park
Finchampstead, RG40 4HT

National Asthma Campaign
Level 1,
Palmerston Crescent
South Melbourne
VIC 3205
Australia

Index

© 2000 Franklin Watts

Franklin Watts
96 Leonard Street
London
EC2A 4XD

Franklin Watts Australia
14 Mars Road
Lane Cove
NSW 2066

ISBN: 0 7496 3800 1

Dewey Decimal Classification
Number: 362.4

10 9 8 7 6 5 4 3 2 1

A CIP catalogue record for
this book is available from the
British Library.

Printed in Malaysia

Consultants: The National Asthma Campaign;
Beverley Matthias (REACH)
Editor: Samantha Armstrong
Designer: Louise Snowdon
Photographer: Chris Fairclough
Illustrator: Eliz Hüseyin

With thanks to: Dominic Garman and his family,
Matthew Baynham, Maureen Conway and the
Llandrindod Silver Band, and the National Asthma Campaign.